The Lord's Prayer
More than Just a Recital

Toks Balogun

Copyright © 2016 Toks Balogun

All rights reserved.

ISBN:1540816257
ISBN-13: 978-1540816252

DEDICATION

I dedicate this to my loving parents.

Dad, Late Okanola Balogun

And

Mum, Adunni Balogun

I appreciate your love and sacrifice to get me to where I am today.

CONTENTS

	Acknowledgments	i
	Forward	x
	Introduction	1
1	Relationship Matters	Pg 9
2	Positioning yourself to be His Favorite	Pg 25
3	Father in Heaven	Pg 50
4	Hallowed be Thy Name	Pg 58
5	Thy Kingdom Come	Pg 71

ACKNOWLEDGMENTS

It felt like it was never going to be. Imagine having something in your mind over a number of years, and you seem not to get around getting it done for one reason or the other. That was the case with this book. Each time I would try to put pen on paper something would crop up and take me off course. Though determined to write, I needed a push, and that is where my lovely wife Adewumi came in. She has been an inspiration and her support for me over the past years, played a significant role in the publishing of this book. A friend truly used to tell me, thank God for your wife. Indeed, I can say thank you Adewumi, you are indeed a helpmeet, and without your support and constant reminder, I couldn't have completed this book. Thanks for believing in me and all your support over the years.

Some people do not directly push you to do something, but their presence and knowledge that they are there for you at all times can be extremely inspirational. My daughters, Ikeoluwa, Enioluwafe, Ifeoluwakitan, and Ewaoluwa, thank you for being there for me. With you around, there is never a dull moment in my life. You add colors to our home in numerous ways that I cannot describe. Your presence and thoughts of you always give me the desire to be the best that I can be.

I cannot but acknowledge some people who have played a meaningful role in my spiritual journey. Their life and ministry have contributed significantly to my growth spiritually. They led and nurtured me from spiritual infancy to where I am today. Pastor and Pastor Mrs. Olufemi Olumide, you laid a solid foundation of Christian faith for me. I was on the quest to be fed spiritually, and you quenched my thirst. You encouraged me to stop taking spiritual milk and gave me the spiritual meat and bones to crack through your teachings. I do acknowledge you today as always. Pastor and Pastor Mrs. Olufemi Mosuro, your leadership, was an inspiration to me. I learnt humility, dedication and total commitment to the service of the Lord from you. The examples you shared were pivotal in laying the foundation for my Pastoral Ministry.

I cannot fail to mention all the brethren of the Rehoboth Assembly Parishes of RCCG in Doha, Qatar, and Calgary, Canada. I am privileged to have served as Shepherd over you. I do not consider myself to be a great orator, but the desire to reach out to you in every way I could led me to writing. In doing so, I discovered a gift of God upon my life. Thank you for your love, and helping me to find my purpose.

As I conclude this acknowledgment, I cannot but appreciate my spiritual father, Pastor EA Adeboye. Your life and ministry have been an absolute inspiration to many of us that call you Daddy. You have passionately and unselfishly dedicated yourself wholly to the service of the Lord and in so doing, impacted many lives, including mine. Thank you, Daddy, for everything you have given to the Kingdom of God.

Lastly, I give all glory to the Lord Almighty, who took me from the miry clay of sin and found me worthy of the grace of adoption as a son. The wisdom, the strength and the inspiration to author a book dedicated to You, my Father comes first of all, from You and You alone. Indeed, You alone are worthy to be praised.

FORWARD

It is not unusual that we get familiar with a route and we drive it mindlessly without paying attention to the road or its signs, there are words that we tend to become familiar and learn like a rote to the point that the essence is lost on us. In this book, Toks takes us through the journey of moving beyond recitation to experiencing the power of God and becoming like Jesus of whom it was said: "He spoke like one with authority". He challenges us to value our relationship with God as it determines what conversation we can have with Him.

Knowing that we live in a generation where God is neither acknowledged nor embraced and we accommodate the clichés and fading fashions of the world, the message in this book brings us back to the basics and simplicity of our relationship with God.

As you read this book, you will learn about praying not as a ritual but as a way of life and encouraged by the lives of others who in their lives saw prayer as an essential part of who they were.

I recommend this book to you as I know its golden nuggets will be a nourishment to your soul and God will bring you a new revelation as you read.

Ask and it shall be given to you.

'Biyi Adeniran

INTRODUCTION

Discovering the Treasure

Growing up was fun, and I had my hands full of the lot that came my way. I liked to explore new things and was very competitive in all that I undertook. The competitive streak might have come from my dad who developed the subtle but evident drive to excel in my sibling and myself. To him, it was not good to be good enough; you needed to be on the top of everything you do. And that apparently still translates to everything I do, the will to excel and be the best comes naturally to me. Thus, at school, I did not want to play catch-up. And if I was made an example of, it was for a good reason, not the opposite. My parents would always say, remember your parents and that stuck with me and defines how I want to be seen.

Coupled with these values, my growing up was shaped by my personal search for a spiritual identity at a very young age. Like most kids growing up at that time, I had an early introduction to God as the creator of all things. I could remember how I used to engage my young mind with varied questions on the personality of God. *I can't help asking myself this question so many times; if my parents birthed me, and they were birthed by theirs, and so forth and so on, then how did God come to be? One simple and an innocent question I always asked as a child was, "Who birthed God?"* I firmly believe that I was not the only one pondering over this question since a very young age. You might have also contemplated along this line of thought as well as a kid or maybe even as an adult. It is human to have a curious mind that seeks an answer to all things. We have asked questions historically; we are asking today, and we will continue to ask in future. I mused on these questions as at that young age, though I did not have the opportunity of reading the scriptures myself, but I had the privilege of being taught the scriptures. How could that be? You might want to ask me.

Despite being born into an Islamic family, I went to an Elementary School established by Missionaries. Even though the school was no longer administered by Missionaries, the inherent values and the educational structure was still very much rooted in the missionary foundation established by the founders. Thus, we were exposed to a considerable level of biblical teachings and values. This elucidates how I got the initial knowledge of scriptures while I was yet to read even a chapter of the Bible.

I still fondly recollect that one of our early morning "rituals" in the assembly gathering before the start of classes was the recitation of some verses of the scriptures, and one that often came repeatedly was the Lord's Prayer. ***To me then, it was just a recital, something I had to memorize because anyone could be called to lead it in the Assembly Hall, and you dare not miss a line because of the non-palatable consequence that awaits you.*** For me the effort to know it stemmed from two things; the spirit to excel in me and to avoid punishment. I couldn't imagine missing a line if I was called to lead the whole assembly in the recital. I knew every word of this scripture, even though I did not know where it was in the Bible, what it meant, how it came about and its value to me. I also saw it as just another recital that I needed to know to bluff about with friends.

However, when I became a Christian and began my personal study of the Scripture, my perspective about prayer completely altered. I didn't want to pray without expecting a response, because I understood, prayer in the real sense of it, is communication with God. I also observed with other people who were praying that it seemed like their requests were not being answered. Nothing was happening in a measure commensurate to the efforts that they would put into the prayers. This led to many becoming despondent in their prayer life. I wondered, why for some people prayer has become a rigorous task while some have not only found joy in praying but also seem to have wonderful testimonies of God's faithfulness through answered prayers. In many instances, unanswered prayers have led many to believe that there is no God, and many have resorted to self-help out of frustration. From this, I concluded that there is something, which the people are doing amiss with their prayers.

This led me back to the Lord's Prayer. The difference from my elementary school days is that now I know the context in which the Lord's Prayer was recorded. It came in answer to a request. The Apostles asked the Lord Jesus Christ to teach them to pray. The Lord's Prayer came in response to that request. Thus, I asked, ***"what is it about the way the Lord taught us to pray? Why did he advise us to pray that way? What set this prayer apart? I came to the realization that this is not just a recital; it is much more than knowing the words of this scripture. It is the whole essence of the relationship between man and God. It is not only about man's expectations; it is also about God's expectations."*** I concluded with the understanding that the Lord's Prayer is a treasure, a hidden treasure waiting to be mined. No wonder the scripture says in Proverbs 2:1-5.

> *"My son, if thou wilt receive my words, and hide my commandments with thee; So, that thou incline thine ear unto wisdom, and apply thine heart to understanding; Yea, if thou criest after knowledge, and liftest up thy voice for understanding; If thou seekest her as silver, and searchest for her as for hid treasures; [5] Then shalt thou understand the fear of the LORD, and find the knowledge of God."*

Reading the Lord's Prayer was pleasurable to me, and for many, it could have been the same. However, the reality is that it's much more than just another recital, it is life, a hidden treasure waiting to be uncovered. I was proud that I knew how to rehearse it when I was a child but now am blessed that I have discovered the real meaning of it as a Christian. I hold and cherish it as an invaluable treasure. To all that want to uncover the power of communicating with God, the Lord Jesus Christ gave it in response to the Apostles request. Interestingly unlike me when I was much younger, many are in the Church today, they are very familiar with the Lord's prayer, they know where it is in the Bible, they can recite it, but they have understood the faith only till this peripheral level. Unfortunately, this applies to many parts of the scripture.

You Desire to Pray? Dare to Ask How

So, do you have the desire to pray? Or maybe I should ask, do you want to provoke the power of prayer? Have you seen the manifestation of answered prayer in the life of others and wondered, why is mine different? Let me say this to you, you are not alone. Not only in this present world, even long before now, people have searched for answers to these puzzles but it has seemingly remained an unsolved riddle for them. Although, it doesn't have to be like that for you. The disciples of the Lord Jesus Christ also had this puzzle ringing through their minds. They saw him pray so many times and witnessed the manifestation of answered prayers, so they also desired a similar miracle in their prayer lives. Thus, they dared to ask, ***"Lord teach us to pray, just as John taught his disciples".*** The Lord's replied with what is today called the Lord's Prayer, which, for generations, many have learned to memorize and recite.

Discovering the treasure in the Lord's Prayer was eye opening and life transforming for me. Do you want to find this treasure just like I did? Each volume of this book gives an exposition on the Lord's Prayer. It takes you beyond the letters of the Holy Scripture to the spirit behind it. It brings about the understanding that could change your perspective not just about this verses of the scripture, but every word that is written in the words of God. Here is your treasure, are you ready to go for it?

Our Father which art in heaven, Hallowed be thy name. Thy kingdom come, thy will be done on earth, as it is in heaven. Give us this day our daily bread. And forgive us our debts, as we forgive our debtors. And lead us not into temptation, but deliver us from evil: For thine is the kingdom, and the power, and the glory, forever. Amen.

CHAPTER ONE

RELATIONSHIP MATTERS

Let me share with you a narrative of an experience, which I felt during a large worship event some years back.

That night, as I walked back towards my room after the worship program I was basking in the glory of my recent experience. The experience had demonstrated the power of God and I was personally moved by it. All I wanted to do was to get back to my room as soon as I could and have a good rest. But that particular night, it was taking me longer than I had imagined. The crowd seems to be walking in the opposite direction to me. I considered the option of turning back, to take a seat for a while in the worship arena, and allow the crowd to disperse before I take a walk back to the accommodation area. The moment, I turned back, this thought quickly disappeared. You will ask me why? I realized, either way, I turn, I shall be walking against the traffic. Turning back will not be a good idea after all.

Mingling my way through the sea of legs, I prayed silently to the Lord. "Oh, Lord, you can see the crowd that has come to meet you. Please meet each one of them at every point when they need you, and answer their prayers. Oh Lord." I sincerely prayed for each of the faithful, as I made my way through the crowd. But you know what? I got an immediate response from the Lord. It was one of those graceful days when God did not wait too long to respond to my prayers. Albeit, not the kind of response I was expecting. Do you know what God blessed me with, in my heart as I said that prayer? ***"They did not come to meet with me; they have not come to me," he said again. They have come to meet with their Pastor"***. That response took me aback, I was perplexed, and surprised at the same time. However, the more I pondered on it during that short distance to my room, the more I discovered the heart of God in the place of prayer. The Lord enlightened me with a new perspective on praying and showed a guiding light to his expectations from us when we seek his face. You probably wonder, what are those expectations? I invite you to come along on this spiritual journey as I share these thoughts...

The Old and The New Way

The practice in the Old Testament by the children of Israel was to consult God through the Prophets of the time. Now, let me say this upfront, as I need you to get this right. ***The people believed in God; they acknowledged him as a powerful God; they knew he can do what they asked of him. However, they related to him from a distance.*** Their relationship with him was not direct and individual but it was nurtured, cultivated and routed through the Prophets. The Prophets, in turn, carried the responsibility to keep themselves in a position where they can continually relate with God. Thus, it is the obligation of the Prophet or High Priest to maintain a relationship with God so he can intercede on behalf of the people. This understanding explains why they were constantly at odds with the Lord. That also relates why Elijah thought he was the only Prophet to not emulate the way of the Baal. The Holy Scripture shows that Elijah's reference was not to the people; it was to the Prophets of his time when he said he alone was left.

"And he said, I have been very jealous for the LORD God of hosts: for the children of Israel have forsaken thy covenant, thrown down thine altars, and slain thy prophets with the sword;

and I, even I only, am left; and they seek my life, to take it away." 1 Kings 19:14

This perspective is also quite common in many cultures of the world today. The Priests in many traditional religions function as the medium or the bridge between men and the gods. The masses come to the Priest or Spiritualist to consult with the gods on their behalf. In the majority of cases, it is seen that they have no relationship with the gods being consulted. The Priests have a functional obligation to keep the communication flowing between the gods and men. The followers are a third party in this arrangement. Are you following my line of thought here?

God made me understand that in the present times, this same old approach is the norm in several Christian gatherings. ***Do we believe in God? Yes, we do. Do we believe in his supernatural power? Yes, we do. Do we desire the miraculous power? Surely, we do. Do we have a good relationship with him? No, we don't always.*** We expect the Pastors to take responsibility and be accountable for that while we most often care less about our day to day living with God. We relate to God as a third party in our relationship with him and by extension, in our prayer life. But is this the expectation of the loving God from his faithful followers? **NO**. In fact, he made us understand in his word in ***Heb.***

11:6 that, "Anyone that comes to God must not only believe that He is and that He is a rewarder...", but God also expects in that seeking, we should be diligent. That doesn't seem like a third-party affair to me, does it to you?

Now, you may ask me, what is the "New" part of the relationship with God? Do you know that the veil separating the Holy of Holies in the temple was divided into two as the Lord finished his work on the cross of Calvary? Is the significance of this event lost on us? Maybe I could remind us the sacrosanct implication of this event. The Lord, by the death of his only son, granted us direct access to his throne of grace, while also recognizing the expectations of God even as we come to his presence. This realization is the "New."

But it is high time we ask ourselves why are we still stuck in the old way, why do we still treat God as a third party in our prayer life? Let me point this out to you, to have a productive prayer life, your personal relationship with God matters. The relationship your Pastor, Reverend or Bishop or whoever is the spiritual head of your Church has with the Lord is simply not sufficient. No. Your own personal relationship is paramount. That is why the scriptures say *"the effectual fervent prayer of a righteous man availeth much"* James 5:16b KJV. The key word here is righteous, which denotes the personal relationship the individual has with God. Remember, the Apostles had a relationship with The Lord Jesus Christ, yet when they asked him, teach us to pray, he pointedly told them, "Pray thus… **OUR FATHER."**

Our Father

I have invested time to emphasize the importance of the relationship with God in our prayer life in order to bring in focus the significance of the opening statement in the Lord's Prayer, **"OUR FATHER."** The Lord Jesus Christ in response to his disciples' request to teach them how to pray accentuated the need for a defining individual relationship between man and God. That, to me, is the starting point. This is not just another ordinary relationship, and cannot be equated to the relationship between brothers and sisters, friends and acquaintances, boss and subordinates. No, it is much more than that, it is a relationship of father to a child.

Have you ever asked someone for help and the individual turned down your request? Have you ever measured how your relationship with a person influences the level of your expectations? Or maybe, let's reverse the role. How does it feel if someone you care about asks you for something and you could respond positively to such a request? Satisfied? Fulfilled? You will agree with me that our disposition to approach an individual for a request or respond to the request of someone is influenced by the level of our relationship with that person. Also, the state of that relationship at the time of asking would influence the response. That context of relationship was emphasized be the Lord Jesus Christ when he responded to the Cannanite woman in Matthew 15:26; "it is not meet to take the children's bread, and to cast it to the dogs".

With these in mind, let's put into context, the relationship between a father and the child. And as we do that, let's try to outline the lessons we must learn as we approach God, the Father in prayer as a child.

Lesson 1

Are you His Child? Who Said So, You or Him?

"Nevertheless, the foundation of God standeth sure, having this seal: "The Lord knoweth those who are His," and, "Let everyone who nameth the name of Christ depart from iniquity." 2 Tim 2:19

Your identity in Christ is not something that you alone can declare. Anybody can claim to be a child of God, but only God can say who truly belong to him. What is undeniably apparent from the Lord's Prayer is the fact that there is a way God wants to see us, children, and there is a way He wants us to see him, father. This is the foundation of prayer. It is a foundation that is built on the very essence of a relationship. In absence of this foundation, one may take the wrong step forward. This understanding is what the Lord Jesus Christ wants us to have when we pray. Can you imagine how many people are on the wrong path and are still taking the wrong steps even today? Many are wailing over unanswered prayers and pointing fingers, not knowing that they must look inward and ask, "Am I a child of God? If I think I am his child, does he see me that way?" That is a food for thought.

The question you may want to ask is, who is a child of God? In John 1vs.12 (KJV), the Bible says,

"But as many as received him, to them gave the power to become the sons of God, even to them that believe on his name." That sounds simple, doesn't it? All I have to do is to believe that Jesus is the son of God, and I also become one. But, is it really that simple? No, I don't think so. You know something? This is where a lot of people get it wrong in their relationship with God. It is more than only what you say through your words. I will attempt to break this scripture down for you for a better understanding.

There are two comprehending parts to this verse of the scripture. One is to receive or accept the personality of God, and the other is to believe in the name of God. It is possible to acknowledge the authority a name carries without necessarily taking on that individual's values or opinion. For example, if someone knows that mentioning the name of a person in authority can influence a decision in their favor, they use that name. It does not necessarily translate into the acceptance of the personality represented by that name. It is nothing more but simply a means to an end. A scriptural example of this can be seen in the life of the Seven Sons of Sceva as recorded in Acts 19 vs. 16-20 (KJV)

"And God wrought special miracles by the hands of Paul: So that from his body were brought unto the sick handkerchiefs or aprons, and the diseases departed from them, and the

evil spirits went out of them. Then certain of the vagabond Jews, exorcists, took upon them to call over them which had evil spirits the name of the LORD Jesus, saying, We adjure you by Jesus whom Paul preacheth. And there were seven sons of one Sceva, a Jew, and chief of the priests, which did so. And the evil spirit answered and said, Jesus I know, and Paul I know; but who are ye? And the man in whom the evil spirit was leaped on them, and overcame them, and prevailed against them so that they fled out of that house naked and wounded."

Instead of glory, the Sons of Sceva suffered shame, instead of being victors, they became victims. You know why? They used the Almighty's name without having received Jesus. They had no authority to use the name and this was the underlying difference between them and Apostle Paul. Paul was not just using the name of Jesus; he had received Jesus in his life. The question is, have you? Yes, you can go on your knees and pray in the name of Jesus because you believe in that powerful name. You have seen the power in the name of Jesus as manifested in the life of others. You have heard testimony being shared on the supremacy of his name. But, let me tell you this, it goes beyond that, for the simple reason that the father knows his children. That is why he said in 2 Timothy 2 vs. 19. He knows who are his own.

"Not everyone that saith unto me, Lord, Lord, shall enter into the kingdom of heaven; but he that doeth the will of my Father which is in heaven. Many will say to me in that day, Lord, Lord, have we not prophesied in thy name? and in thy name have cast out devils? and in thy name done many wonderful works? And then will I profess unto them, I never knew you: depart from me, ye that work iniquity." Matt 7:21-23

So, with this understanding, as you go to the Lord in prayer, the question to ask yourself is, do I see myself as a child of God, and, has he accepted me as his own? This is one key lesson the Lord want us to learn as he taught us how to pray.

Lesson 2

A Child is Dependent on The Father

For as long as you see yourself as a child in the presence of God, you will have an absolute dependence on him. Thus, it can be spiritually rewarding if your attitude in prayers and in the presence of God is that of submission. You do not want to impose your will but rely on the guidance and judgment of the father. This attitude gives you a high latitude before God. In the book of Luke 22 vs. 42, the Lord Jesus Christ prayed and said, Father, if thou be willing, remove this cup from me: nevertheless, not my will, but thine, be done. This demonstrates an example of a child who is utterly dependent on the father.

As a child, we must recognize that it was not every time we ask our father for something, that they provide it to us, not because they don't have it, but because they know better and want to inculcate a sense of accountability in the child. During my childhood, if my Dad had given me everything I had requested for, I am very sure I will not be where I am today. Our parents used their knowledge and judgment to determine what can be provided to us. That is why the Scripture says in James 4 vs. 3 (KJV): *Ye ask, and receive not, because ye ask amiss, that ye may consume it upon your lusts.* **You must not only be willing to present your requests to the Lord, but you must**

also be humble enough to accept his response. And I tell you from experience, it could either be Yes or No. According to the Holy Scripture, when the Lord Jesus finished praying in the Garden of Gethsemane, an Angel came to strengthen him (Luke 22:41-43). My understanding of the instance is that he needed strength to accept the response of God. ***Being strengthened in the place of prayer does not necessary mean the grace to pray for a long time, but also the ability to accept the response from God.***

So, ask yourself these questions, and answer honestly. Are you entirely dependent on him? Is it about your will or his will? Are you ready to accept his response? You must be conscious of this as you approach God in prayer.

Lesson 3:

The Father is Responsible for The Child:

"Therefore, I say unto you, take no thought for your life, what ye shall eat, or what ye shall drink; nor yet for your body, what ye shall put on. Is not the life more than meat, and the body than raiment? Behold the fowls of the air: for they sow not, neither do they reap nor gather into barns; yet your heavenly Father feedeth them. Are ye not much better than they? Which of you by taking thought can add one cubit unto his stature? And why take ye thought for raiment? Consider the lilies of the field, how they grow; they toil not, neither do they spin: And yet I say unto you, that even Solomon in all his glory was not arrayed like one of these. Wherefore, if God so clothe the grass of the field, which to day is, and tomorrow is cast into the oven, shall he not much more clothe you, O ye of little faith? Therefore, take no thought, saying, what shall we eat? or, what shall we drink? or, Wherewithal shall we be clothed? For after all these things do the Gentiles seek:) for your heavenly Father knoweth that ye have need of all these things."

Here, the scripture implies that you don't have to tell me about my responsibilities. I am completely aware of my obligations and I am capable of living up to my accountabilities to you.

This all-giving position of God was further emphasized by the statement that if God can take care of the needs of the grass of the field and the birds of the air, he would surely take complete care of the needs of those he has made in his own image.

Are you still in doubt about how this could be? Let us take a reference from the scripture to bring this home to you. In the Book of 1 Kings 17, Elijah had just proclaimed to King Ahab that there will be famine in the Land. It was not only the King that heard it, but God also heard it and supported Elijah. However, he did not stop at causing the famine, but he made provision for Elijah so that he will not be a victim of the impending famine. Hear what the Scripture says from Vs. 2.

"And the word of the LORD came unto him, saying, Get thee hence, and turn thee eastward, and hide thyself by the brook Cherith, that is before Jordan. And it shall be, that thou shalt drink of the brook; and I have commanded the ravens to feed thee there. So he went and did according unto the word of the LORD: for he went and dwelt by the brook Cherith, that is before Jordan. And the ravens brought him bread and flesh in the morning, and bread and flesh in the evening; and he drank of the brook"
1 Kings 17:2

Did you notice that Elijah did not even once query God on how he will be able to feed during the famine period? God knew he has to be taken care of, and so he made a provision for Elijah. That is the nature of the father you are praying to, he knows what you need, and he will not shun away from his responsibility to provide for you. You must have this understanding as you approach the Lord in prayer.

And you know what? That is not all, there is more to this father than the ordinary. Let's flip over to the next chapter as we embark on a journey of discovery on how you can position yourself to receive divine attention from **"Our Father."**

CHAPTER TWO

POSISTIONING YOURSELF TO BE HIS FAVOURITE

The attributive adjective in the Lord's Prayer, "Our" should not be overlooked and disregarded. It points us to a meaningful reality that we must recognize when we pray. The Lord prayer could have started with "My father." I earnestly believe that the use of the word "Our" is to bring to our consciousness an important understanding that should be obvious to each one of us. The idea that you are not the only one seeking his divine attention. Analogous to you, others are praying, as well. Just like he is responsible for you, so he is, for many others as well. Thus, it becomes all the more imperative for us to position ourselves in such a way among the multitude of faithful that we are looked at favorably by him. Let me ask you a question, how about positioning yourself to be his favorite? Would you find that appealing? Would this proposition interest you?

The consequent question then is, how does one become God's favorite? How can I be singled out from the masses? These are questions that are bound to intrigue and interest everyone who desires a fulfilling prayer life. In the last Chapter, we established the fact that prayer starts with a relationship. Here, I want us to take it a step further by perceiving and putting into focus the significance of the Lord Jesus Christ not personalizing the father-child relationship while teaching us to pray by using the phrase "Our Father" instead of "My Father." However, before we delve further into this, let me quickly reemphasize that God the father is responsible for each and every one of his children. Herein, I am attempting to explore and direct attention to the fact that apart from the primary responsibility of parents to a child, we can set ourselves apart for much more than the ordinary. Let us not forget that the Bible says in James 5:16b "...*the effectual fervent prayer of a righteous man availeth much.*" The implication of this is the probable ineffectiveness of prayer, which could lead to frustration and disenchantment with God, the father. This miserable situation can be avoided if we have a proper understanding of this special father-child relationship.

So, how do I get you started on this path? Let me use an analogy of myself. I am not an only child, I grew up with many siblings, and with that, I know what it means to seek the attention of my parents. They certainly loved every one of us equally, and they showed that affection at all times. However, we are also not oblivious to the fact that certain things can ensure us the listening ears of our parent. And the more we are in their good books, the more we are positioned to get their attention, sometimes taking advantage of the other siblings while doing so. I believe we can all relate to this reality either as a child growing up or perhaps as parents. This dynamics of relationship management can be equated to the nature of our relationship with God.

This brings us to the desired consciousness we must have as we approach the Lord in prayer. We are not the only one seeking his attention, and you need to know that several others are making the same request as you in their prayers. Thus, you need to place yourself in a favorable way that you have his listening ear. This we must essentially appreciate as we approach the Lord in prayers. That is why Prophet Isaiah says in the Book of Isaiah 59:1-2

"Behold, the LORD's hand is not shortened, that it cannot save; neither his ear heavy that it cannot hear: But your iniquities have separated between you and your God, and your sins have hid his face from you, that he will not hear."

We must, therefore, learn to advantageously position ourselves as God's favorites to reap the full benefits of prayers. You may want to ask if God has favorites. The simple response I have for you is, do you have favorites? If your answer is yes, then remember, you are made in God-likeness and image. Simply implying that your attributes reflect the attributes of God.

"And God said, Let us make man in our image, after our likeness: and let them have dominion over the fish of the sea, and over the fowl of the air, and over the cattle, and over all the earth, and over every creeping thing that creepeth upon the earth. So God created man in his own image, in the image of God created he him; male and female created he them." Gen 1:26-27

Here, I must also share with you that not being a favorite doesn't imply you are not his child. However, it does mean that you are not well positioned. And certainly during a prayer, you do not want to be unfavorably positioned. This leads us to the question, as to how can one ensure to be in an advantageous position before God as we approach him in prayer? We must know the answer to this question as we pray. It is also important to emphasize that this is not about what you must do to obtain salvation. No, far from it. That is a free gift of grace granted through the blood of the Lamb, and not affected by your work. The essence of my discourse here is that a child may not have a say or control on the choice of the family of birth, but the child can surely work towards developing a positive and endearing relationship with the parents.

There are several examples in the scriptures where God has demonstrated that he feels very personal and well-disposed to certain individuals. There are diverse qualities and issues that differentiate those people from the milieu. If we must position ourselves as God's favorites, I think the good way to start is to look and learn from the life of these individuals. What do they have that distinguishes them in the eyes of God?

Abraham, a man of faith

One of the most intriguing questions I have asked myself in my personal study of the Bible is "Why did God choose Abraham over every other person in his time?" This forms the main idea discussed in detail in another book of mine, but we cannot at this stage not look at the life of Abraham as we consider the subject of God's favorites. Doing that will be ignoring the importance of what God said in Genesis 18...***there is nothing I want to do that I can hide from Abraham, having known him, he delights me and am assured as well he will pass on what I have shared with him to generations that are coming after him***. *(My paraphrase of Genesis 18: 17-19)*

This embodies absolute trust. In present times we can say Abraham was God's confidante. We need to consider, "How did Abraham endear himself so much to God, to an extent that God shares his private thought with him?" God had absolute faith in Abraham. ***He talked about how Abraham would manage his children even when he had no child at the time. His perception of him was not about who he was, but what he will become, Father of many Nations. Should that surprise you? No. I don't think so. Our God perceives differently than man. God is not about the physical, He is about the heart. God is not only about the present, He***

Is also about the future. It also means that it doesn't matter where you are now if you have faith in God, there is no limit to the heights and the horizons to which he can take you. God is not leading you, or interested in you based on your current status, but based on how you can grow in him and with him. If you are walking with God, you should be concerned more about your future than your present.

Though this book does not focus on the subject of faith, however, we cannot talk about prayer without mentioning faith. For you to be God's favorite, you must believe in him. For a productive prayer life, it is imperative for you to have unshakable and absolute faith in God.

"But without faith it is impossible to please him: for he that cometh to God must believe that he is, and that he is a rewarder of them that diligently seek him." Heb 11:6

"For therein is the righteousness of God revealed from faith to faith: as it is written, The just shall live by faith" Roman 1:17

Abraham's walk with God started the same way many start their journey with God today, or maybe even back in Abraham's time. But when we speak of faith we cannot talk about many other faithful as about Abraham. This sets him apart and that is why he is called the father of faith, today. His walk of faith with God started when he was summoned to advance towards an unknown place. He left everything and followed God's instruction, even though he knew not where he was heading and what awaits him there. The Bible describes Abraham not as an ordinary man, struggling to survive but he was a successful and well-established individual. He, however, left everything and did as per God's will. Abraham can be likened to a successful businessman who walked away from his investment to start an uncertain new life. It takes strong faith to make such a tough decision.

"By faith Abraham, when he was called to go out into a place which he should after receive for an inheritance, obeyed; and he went out, not knowing whither he went." Heb 11:8

This disposition endeared Abraham to the Lord. As we read in Hebrews 11:6a (KJV), **But without faith, it is impossible to please God.** It, therefore, goes to say that, if you fail to please him, you cannot be his favorite and if not, you are not well positioned when you are offering your prayer.

Coming back to the discussion that led to the Lord's Prayer, the Apostle realized that they were not having the same results as the Lord Jesus Christ when he would pray. Therefore, they asked

Jesus to teach them to pray. Also, there are several instances in the Bible, where the Lord emphasizes the importance of faith in making our request known to the Lord.

"Therefore, I say unto you, what things whatsoever ye desire, when ye pray, believe that ye receive them, and ye shall have them." Mark 11:24

"And Jesus said unto them, Because of your unbelief: for verily I say unto you, If ye have faith as a grain of mustard seed, ye shall say unto this mountain, Remove hence to yonder place; and it shall remove; and nothing shall be impossible unto you." Mathew 17:20

Thus, accessing God's abundance and favor in prayers is a function of our faith. As I close on this point, let me share with you a testimony to demonstrate the power of having faith in God.

A faith-based program was being organized in a black dominated Church, in London. It was meant specifically for those believing and praying to God for the fruit of the womb – child. A Caucasian lady got to the Church during the Pastor's teaching, she was late as the program had started much earlier. Surprisingly, not quite five minutes had she sat down, she stood up and headed for the exit door. The Pastor was startled and felt maybe he had said something offensive and that was why the lady was leaving. Being Caucasian as well, some of the Volunteers felt that she might not be too comfortable in the midst of a black dominated congregation. The volunteers tried to influence her to stay but she was not having any of it, so she left. About six months later, the lady was back in the Church and, this time, no one could connect her back to the event of six months earlier. You know why? She was heavily pregnant. It was time for testimony, and she also stood up to share hers as well. And here is what she had to say.

"You probably may not recognize me. About six months ago I was in this Church. Not because I was invited by anyone, but I was on my way home from work when I saw the flyers of a program being organized for those believing God for Childbirth. That was my unfortunate situation at that time as I had been married without a child for a while. I decided to come for the program since the venue was along my route. On getting to the Church, some few minutes after I sat down, the Pastor said, "Tonight is somebody's night. The Lord will answer your prayers tonight." As soon as I heard that, I looked at my wristwatch to check the time. I knew if it was to be my night, I had to leave the Church right away. I knew the time my husband goes to bed and if I do not leave at that minute, I will not be home before he goes to bed. I believed what the Pastor said that it was my night and I needed to make it my night. The volunteers tried to stop me from leaving, but nobody could stop me at that time as I was determined to get home in time before my husband went to bed. Thankfully, I got home on time and that night God answered our prayers of many years. Today I am pregnant with a baby, the result of that night's act of faith."

That was faith at work. Do you know how many people would have attended that event in the same condition as that lady without experiencing any breakthrough in their condition? They would have left thinking that God had not been present in that program as nothing happened in their case. But it is not so and reminds me of the story in Book of Mark Chapter 2. Four men wanted to see Lord Jesus for the healing of their sick friend and were not ready to return without seeing Jesus. So, they broke the ceiling to present their friend to the Lord. The Bible said the Lord saw their faith and healing came upon the man. Was he the only one sick at the place, probably not. But it was their faith that the Lord saw, and it individualized from the crowd. One thing that can mark you apart from the crowd seeking the Lord is your faith. Remember, the scriptures say, if you have faith as small as the mustard seed, you will move the Mountain. So, are you ready now to move your Mountain? Exercise your faith in the father and become his favorite today. The Bible says

Abraham believed in the Lord and earned his righteousness in the eyes of God.

Job, a Devout Worshiper

Is the Lord proud of you? Can he proudly identify with you amongst many? While you ruminate and meditate on that, let me introduce to you someone God proudly identified with.

"Now there was a day when the sons of God came to present themselves before the LORD, and Satan came also among them. And the LORD said unto Satan, Whence comest thou? Then Satan answered the LORD, and said, From going to and fro in the earth, and from walking up and down in it. And the LORD said unto Satan, Hast thou considered my servant Job, that there is none like him in the earth, a perfect and an upright man, one that feareth God, and escheweth evil?" Job 1:6-8

The man Job is a classic example of someone God was immensely proud of and even boasted about him to the devil. God spoke of him as someone that could not be compared to others when it comes to his devotion to him. The devil's response to God was simple. He said, Job is devoted to you because of what he could derive from the relationship and if this benefit is taken away, he would surely deny you. What follows is the greatest human trial recorded in the Bible. Job lost his entire fortune and his children in quick succession. But he defiantly refused to give up his faith and his relationship with God, despite the pressure mounted on him by the people around him, including his wife.

"Though he slay me, yet will I trust in him: but I will maintain mine own ways before him. He also shall be my salvation: for an hypocrite shall not come before him." Job 13:15-16

There are many lessons that we can learn from Job's enduring faith, but there is one that stands out for me. When the devil is right about the negative motive of your relationship with God, most likely you are one of his several favorites, but when God speaks for your uprightness, you are one of his very few favorites.

God knew Job's devotion to him was not based on material benefits, but it was genuine love and interest in God. The devil was wrong when he assumed it was a tradeoff because of what God was bestowing on him. Would you like to pray this prayer with me?

May the devil be constant in getting it wrong about me. Amen.

The affirmation of God on Job was that he was not pretentious towards him. Even though Job had not faced any challenges and stressful experience prior to this, God knew his heart. God was aware that any adverse situation could not deter him from loving him and singled him out as an uncommon worshiper. Job himself had a deep love for God and knew that it is not profitable to be a hypocrite before God. So, if you want to be a favorite of your father, what you should not be is a hypocrite. Don't present yourselves the way you are not, because God knows you more than you can imagine.

And The Sweat Gave Me Away

Talking about being a hypocrite, a throwback to my younger age will help you in gaining an insight. I had many rough rides with my Dad during my growing up years. He was a strict disciplinarian and expected a lot from every child under his roof. The rules were clear, and if you break them, you knew that you must face the consequences. Sometimes, in a bit to express myself, as many of us do, I had my share of the rough rides. I cannot forget a particular experience, which happened when I was about twelve years old. I loved playing street football, and as my Dad would not allow it. Thus, I always look out for every opportunity to get involved when my parents were not around. On this particular day, to prevent myself from getting caught playing street football, I had informed my friends to alert me if they see my Dad's car coming from afar on the street. Unfortunately, the information came while we were deep into the game. I made a quick dash home and straight away went to my room. I started to read, pretending as if I was not out of the house. That was the way my Dad met me; that was where I wanted him to meet me, at my desk reading. As I greeted him, he smiled, and I thought I have won the battle of wits. However, he asked me a simple question, "Why are you sweating heavily?" At that moment, I looked at myself, I was full of sweat, which obviously could not have been from sitting and reading. I knew right away that the sweat has given me away, and you can easily guess what followed. Also, the event of that day limited my ability to approach him for anything for some days.

I believe many of us can relate to the above scenario. We sometimes try to present ourselves in a particular way to achieve a set objective, which in most cases leads to deception. This attitude also applies to our relationship with God; you cannot be a hypocrite and be a favorite of God. The Bible says, "God is a Spirit: and they that worship him must worship him in spirit and in truth." We limit our opportunities in prayers when our devotion is not complete and when we choose what to obey and what not to. Remember what the Lord told Cain, "***If thou doest well, shall thou not be accepted?" Gen 4:7a.*** He was there to offer his sacrifice just like his brother, but his sacrifice was rejected while Abel's was accepted. Why? Because God is not only looking at what is presented, but also at the heart that is presenting.

So, are you a devout worshiper? Or is your relationship with God influenced by some other considerations? Do you just love him for who he is or because of what he has? If the dynamics change, will you still declare your love for him? You must positively answer these questions if you want God to single you out as he did Job. As I close on this issue, I will leave you to meditate on the scripture in the book of Romans 8:38-39.

"Who shall separate us from the love of Christ? shall tribulation, or distress, or persecution, or famine, or nakedness, or peril, or sword? As it is written, For thy sake we are killed all the day long; we are accounted as sheep for the slaughter. Nay, in all these things we are more than conquerors through him that loved us. For I am persuaded, that neither death, nor life, nor angels, nor principalities, nor powers, nor things present, nor things to come, Nor height, nor depth, nor any other creature, shall be able to separate us from the love of God, which is in Christ Jesus our Lord."

David, A Man after God's Heart

"And afterward they desired a king: and God gave unto them Saul the son of Cis, a man of the tribe of Benjamin, by the space of forty years. And when he had removed him, he raised up unto them David to be their king; to whom also he gave their testimony, and said, I have found David the son of Jesse, a man after mine own heart, which shall fulfil all my will. Of this man's seed hath God according to his promise raised unto Israel a Saviour, Jesus" Acts 13:21-23

David's ascendancy to the throne was not hereditary. God was looking out for a man with a distinct character, a man after God's heart. A man that is constantly looking out for every opportunity to please God. Someone who can give himself completely to the cause of God. In David, he found such an individual. Even though David was young and not from an affluent family in the society, God saw in him a future King, someone he could rely on to deliver on his mandate, which was a major failure of his predecessor, King Saul.

The appointment of David to Kingship in Israel was an example of God's favor. Indeed, the events that happened during his kingship are also suggestive that David got away with some things that God could have handled in a different way if it was another individual. Yes, Saul disobeyed, he failed to carry out God's instruction to the fullest, and, for this reason, he was dethroned as King. However, the scriptures tell us that David did not only commit adultery, but he also killed his own subject to cover his sin of adultery. Yet the Lord allowed for his throne to remain in Israel forever. That tells me there was a special grace of God upon David which was apparently missing in the life of Saul. So what distinguished David from Saul? What made him unique in the eyes of God? How did he become God's favorite?

There are several instances in the scripture that provide an answer to these questions. However, I will love to start by looking at how David came in the limelight. The encounter with Goliath sheds sufficient light on the personality of David and his heart for God.

"So David rose early in the morning, left the sheep with a keeper, and took the things and went as Jesse had commanded him. And he came to the camp as the army was going out to the fight and shouting for the battle. For Israel and the Philistines had drawn up in battle array, army against army. And David left his supplies in the hand of the supply keeper, ran to the army, and came and greeted his

brothers. Then as he talked with them, there was the champion, the Philistine of Gath, Goliath by name, coming up from the armies of the Philistines; and he spoke according to the same words. So David heard them. And all the men of Israel, when they saw the man, fled from him and were dreadfully afraid. So the men of Israel said, "Have you seen this man who has come up? Surely he has come up to defy Israel; and it shall be that the man who kills him the king will enrich with great riches, will give him his daughter, and give his father's house exemption from taxes in Israel."Then David spoke to the men who stood by him, saying, "What shall be done for the man who kills this Philistine and takes away the reproach from Israel? For who is this uncircumcised Philistine, that he should defy the armies of the living God?" I Sam 17:20-26

Here we see a young man, passionate about God and cannot stand the name of God being mentioned in disrepute. Here we see a young man, who abandoned the cause that posited him at the war front and made the business of God his primary Goal. Here we see a young man who chose to stand for God when others were backing out. And here we see a young man, who was ready to give himself up and put his life on the line because he refused to condone disrespect to his God. Do you really think that David's relationship with God would remain at the same level when he came back from that encounter? Or, let me ask you this, do you think God would have appreciated Saul and his Army the same way as David after he stood up against Goliath and redeemed the name of the Lord? Certainly not. It was not unexpected that David occupied a special place in the heart of God after this feat. It can be likened to just how any father would be proud of a child who has brought glory to his name. David by this encounter started on his journey to the heart of the Lord. Oh, did I hear you say that David was favored because of the anointing on him? Let me remind you, King Saul was anointed as well, but he was unable to take a stand to defend the name of God.

We have established earlier from the scripture that, God has granted everyone who has received him the power to become sons of God. But I must emphasize here that it is one thing to become a child of God and be referred to as such, and it is another to act like a child of God. Saul and his army represented the army of the living God, but their actions were not representative of the actions of a child of God. The same applies to us today. As believers, we are all regarded as children of God, but do we all act like one? If you don't act like his child and you do not represent him well, how do you expect that God would feel about you? In the book of I Samuel 16 vs. 1, God said to Samuel, "For how long will you mourn for

Saul, for I have rejected him." This means that Saul was no longer in the reckoning of God as King over Israel. Can you pray this short prayer...***May I not be lost in the plan of God in Jesus name, Amen.***

But is this all that illustrates how David warmed himself into the heart of God? No, there is much more than that. David was also a very thankful man, who ardently acknowledged God in all his ways. That could explain why more than half of the book of Psalms were authored by him. In Psalms 26:6-7, he said, ***"I wash my hands in innocence, and go about your altar, O LORD, proclaiming aloud your praise and telling of all your wonderful deeds."*** David's attitude of giving thanks and being grateful was a great determining factor in his strong relationship with God. As a young child, I learned early enough to be thankful and appreciate people. And as an adult, I appreciate it when people acknowledge a gift and respond with thanks. In the same manner, God expects us to be thankful and recognize his faithfulness in our lives.

Thanksgiving is a powerful tool in the place of prayer, and that is why Psalmist encourages us to enter His gates with thanksgiving. So, do you want to be God's favorite? Do you want a transformation in your prayer life? Cultivating the attitude of thanksgiving is a good way to start.

As I close this Chapter, let me quickly sum this up by saying that the best way to position yourself in an advantageous position with God "Our Father" is to completely trust and obey him. Abraham, Job, and David, all three had one thing in common, they trusted and obeyed the Lord in entirety. So, I ask, do you trust and obey him? Can you consider yourself his favorite? That reminds me of the hymn by John H. Sammis, the lyrics of that song says much to us today.

When we walk with the Lord in the light of His Word, What a glory He sheds on our way!
While we do His good will, He abides with us still,
And with all who will trust and obey.

Trust and obey, for there's no other way
To be happy in Jesus, but to trust and obey.

Not a shadow can rise, not a cloud in the skies,
But His smile quickly drives it away;
Not a doubt or a fear, not a sigh or a tear,
Can abide while we trust and obey.

Refrain

Not a burden we bear, not a sorrow we share,
But our toil He doth richly repay;
Not a grief or a loss, not a frown or a cross,
But is blessed if we trust and obey.

Refrain

But we never can prove the delights of His love
Until all on the altar we lay;
For the favor He shows, for the joy He bestows,
Are for them who will trust and obey.

Refrain

Then in fellowship sweet we will sit at His feet.
Or we'll walk by His side in the way.
What He says we will do, where He sends we will go; Never fear, only trust and obey.

CHAPTER THREE

FATHER IN HEAVEN

Have you ever asked someone for assistance and he has genuinely responded by saying, "How I wish I could have been in a position to help, I would have loved to be of assistance?" This response expresses certain limitations on the part of that individual. For instance, there are several things that I would like to do for my kids, but I am unable to do so because I have a limited supply of resources. This exemplifies that irrespective how much a father loves a child and how good and pleasant the child has been, the father's ability to meet the needs of the child is constrained by the resources available to him.

This brings me to the significance of the qualification given to the Father in the Lord's Prayer, "Father in Heaven". The Lord Jesus Christ wants us to be conscious of certain significant elements in the Lord's Prayer like:
(1) The personality of the one to whom we are addressing our prayer, (2) the position he occupies, and (3) the power that he wields.
Think about it this way. If given an opportunity to present different requests to the Mayor of City and the President of the Country, would you have the same wish list? You probably would ask based on

the perceived levels of authority which are attributed to the positions that they occupy and the sphere of their influence. Thus, understanding the personality of God is quite relevant in prayer. In absence of this understanding, you can limit the opportunities and privilege available to you in requesting from the Lord. So, when you approach Him in prayers, believe in mind and soul that you are before the one with whom all things are possible, and there is nothing beyond his capabilities. The Bible says in Psalm 24:1 ***"The earth is the Lord's, and the fullness thereof; the world, and they that dwell therein."*** Can you take some time to muse and understand the meaning of this verse? He does not only own the earth; he owns everything that is in it, above and below ground. If it needs digging, he can dig it out for you. If it needs plucking, he can do that for you. And if it requires him to get it from an individual he can, because everything and everyone is His subjects. Let me clarify, that this is not a figment of my imagination, this has been demonstrated relentlessly by the Lord in His words. Let's share some here.

Arise, Go To Zarapath

After he had declared that there would be no rain in the land, Elijah was led to the brook Cherith. Here the Ravens provided him meals and the brook supplied him with water for sustenance. The resultant drought led to a massive famine over the land, with an acute shortage of food everywhere and many families struggled to go by. Meanwhile, in Zarapeth lived a widow with her son, also a victim of the famine. She was in a desperate situation as she was afraid that the next meal could be her last. In her own words, she was to eat her last meal and die. But God looked kindly unto the widow and her son and intervened before she ate the meal. Before you go ahead from here, can you pray this prayer for yourself; ***May the Lord look kindly on me and my family in Jesus name, Amen.*** Have you prayed? Please make sure you say this prayer before you go ahead with the book.

That she may not starve and die with her son, God told Elijah to arise and go and meet this family. That sounds easy, right? No, it is actually more complicated. Elijah was not just hiding in the brook, there was a specific reason as to why he was not in the open. Since Elijah was the cause for the drought and the economic crises that the nation was going through, probably ransom had been placed on his head by King Ahab. Thus, it was a difficult task for Elijah as he would be out of his comfort in the brook and exposed to danger. That was exactly what God did, and caused the brook in which he was hiding to dry up. I have a feeling that had the brook not dried up, Elijah would have resisted the attempt to go to Zarapeth. He would have given God every reason to stay back. I also believe that if God had wanted him to remain in the brook, the brook wouldn't have seized to produce water. So, the brook dried up so that Elijah may meet the need of the widow of Zarapeth and her son. Although Elijah was unaware that when he left the brook he was not going to meet someone for his own needs, he was on assignment to help someone who was on the verge of death.

Sometimes for help in difficult situations, we look around at our spheres of influence, and we give up when we have exhausted such avenues. I believe that was also the case of this poor widow. I assume that she did not simply give up without trying hard to get a way out of her situation. She must have resigned to that decision after all that she tried failed. But God brought to her help someone completely out of her sphere of influence to help her out of that predicament. This is how our Father in Heaven works. That is the amazing magnitude of what he can do for his chosen ones. Therefore, in asking him for anything, don't look at yourself, don't even limit yourself to the people around you, because your father in Heaven is unlimited. Can I agree with you in prayer as you read this? ***The Lord will cause someone to arise on your behalf. That weight that seems too heavy for you to bear shall be lifted off*** *your head. You shall receive a new lease of life in Jesus name. Amen.*

The Coin and the Fish

The Lord even mobilized the fish of the sea to respond to a need, which was raised to the Lord. In Matthew 17, the Lord Jesus Christ told Peter, that to pay the Tax collector, he should pick a fish from the sea. Jesus said that Peter will find a coin in that fish with which he can pay the Tax collector. This incident of God's loving grace tells me everything that God has created can respond to the commandment of the Lord in order that your needs may be met. Why would Peter not respond to his request, even though strange as it seems. Peter must have remembered and recalled his first encounter with the Lord Jesus. He had toiled all night fishing and caught nothing. The Lord asked him to draw his nets in the morning hours and in doing so Peter got a boat-sinking draught.

Help from Unexpected Source

Our father in heaven can also source direct help from an unexpected source. His might can fetch you help from someone that you never expected. In 2 Kings 7, the Bible recorded that there were some Lepers who were staying outside the gate of the city because of their condition. They were not permitted to live within the city walls as they are considered unclean. In such a despairing situation, their sustenance came in the form of relatives and friends, who regularly brought food and other necessary provisions to them. However, at that time, the Syrians had laid siege in the city and no one was able come out of the city to give them provision. Also, there was a scarcity of food in the city because of the siege. The Leprous Men lost hope and to get meal decided to go to the camp of the Syrians. But God had moved earlier and caused the Syrians to flee. So instead of pleading for a meal, they got an abundance of food. They decided to inform the people in the city about the abundance of provision that was left behind by the fleeing Syrian. Thus, they that had been neglected, became the bearers of good news and thus, help came to the people of Samaria from unexpected sources. Who would have thought that the people who had been banished from the city will bring them good tidings? That is how the father in heaven works.

He is the one that can create anything out of nothing. In Genesis 1, the Bible says that the earth was void and without form. There was nothing in it. But out of this nothing, God created everything with his spoken words. Human beings are creative, but we cannot create something out of anything. We need raw materials to generate a new product. But all God needs is himself and whatever he says, so it will be. As you pray, recognize that the one you are praying to is the supreme father in heaven, the one that can create anything out of nothing. Do not limit yourself in the place of prayer. You can never ask for too much that he cannot do because with him all things are possible.

"But Jesus beheld them, and said unto them, with men this is impossible; but with God all things are possible". Matthew. 19:26

Often when we read the scripture but are unable to relate it to our present times. As I close this chapter, let me tell you a story to demonstrate the power of our God even in today's time.

An incident happened in Paris some years back. The parents of two small children left them in their 8th floor apartment and went out. Somehow, one of the children, aged about 18 months old stepped outside in the balcony and in the process, fell off. What a tragedy you would say. One cannot expect an adult to fall from such a height and survive, not to talk about a small child. But the news is that the baby survived. How did that happen you would say? The report has it that there was a coffee shop on the ground floor of the building. This shop had an extended canopy covering visitor's chairs to have coffee. That child did not hit the ground but fell on the canopy that cushioned the impact of the fall and the baby survived. You may wonder, so how did God come in here? Good question. The story does not end there. The coffee shop was not opened at the time of the fall so one would not have expected the canopy to be up that particular time. This is where God comes in. The shop owner had attempted to bring down the canopy the previous night but couldn't as one of the mechanisms failed. So, in frustration they left the canopy on thinking they will fix the next day. Do you see the miracle? God plans far ahead of you and me, and he can go ahead of you to fix the issues in our lives. Relate this back to the story of Elijah and the widow of Zarapath, then you would understand why the scripture says in Hebrews 13:8... ***Jesus Christ, the same yesterday, today and forever.***

CHAPTER FOUR

HALLOWED BY THY NAME

How dare I call him by name?

I grew up in a society where it is considered abnormal and disrespectful to call someone older than you by their first name. The expectation is that you add a prefix such as "Brother" or "Sister" before the name depending on the gender of the person in reference. Going against this norm, makes you sound disrespectful and can earn you rebuke either from that person, or the society as a whole. That is the culture.

But in my house, it was not so, at least in the interaction between my direct siblings and me. My dad was a stringent disciplinarian, very strict and he expected us to respect each other and conduct ourselves in a dignifying way. He, however, did not believe that if you do not add a prefix to your elder sibling's name, you have not shown respect. So, there was a rule in the house, that everybody would call each other by their first name. This seemed odd to many around us and whenever we had family members visiting, this topic was always raised with my Dad.

My elder brother is four years older than me, and I am also four years older to my younger brother. Between us, we felt that there was nothing strange about the way we interacted and referred to ourselves at home. However, when we would have friends and family visiting us, this issue would always come up. Initially, I never bothered about how my brother felt about it, and why should I really? I had someone who should be calling me "Brother" as well but enjoyed shouting my name as if he was there when I was being named. So, who cares how big brother felt about how he was being called? Certainly, not me!

However, as years rolled by and my big brother entered high school, he started to come home with his friends to study together. With no care in this world, I started to address them with their names, like I addressed my brother. But they were not ready to accept that from me. Not only did they ensure that I put the right prefix before their names, they also encouraged my brother to be hard on me so that I would learn how to "respect" him as well. Though at that time, I accepted this reluctantly, later I grew into it. Dad did not like it but he apparently gave in to the pressure and allowed this change. I think his focus was on my brother; as he told my brother to not let this get into his head, keep his feet down and be focused.

You might be wondering as to why am I sharing these events of my life with you and what has this got to do with the Lord's Prayer? Just a moment, allow me to bring you to that point.

I had grown up calling my brother by name, however after getting used to putting a prefix before his name, I found it very odd that I had been addressing him without the prefix in the past. I started to feel like his name was just too big for me to open my mouth and call directly. And anytime I would mistakenly call him by name, I would quickly apologize feeling embarrassed. I also realized that this singular act also changed my perception of his personality, our relationship and my respect for him. Now, he was more revered to me than before. I found that now it was difficult for me to say no to him, and I would readily run errands for him without complaining. I then saw him more as someone who I could run to for help socially and academically. He suddenly became to me then, indeed, a big brother.

That brings me to the next phrase in the Lord's Prayer, "Hallowed be thy name". To hallow means to honor, to make sacred, to dignify, to respect, and to consecrate. In order words, the Lord in teaching us to pray, wants us as his faithful followers to comprehend and understand the weight and glory that his name carries. He wants us to appreciate the holy and sacrosanct consecrated quality of that supreme name. He needs us to be cognizant of the importance of honoring his name at all times.

To emphasize on the significance of the name, I have shared my personal story, which demonstrates how my relationship with my brother changed when I began to give attention to how I addressed him. Similarly, if we understand the magnitude of the impact of honoring his name in our daily life, our prayer life will change for the better considerably. There will be a transformation in our approach which will further change our expectations from him.

So, ask yourself, how revered is his name to you? What emotion comes to your mind and heart when you hear or you mention his name? How protective are you of that most revered name in your day-to-day life? If he is your father, what honor do you bring to his name? That is why the scriptures say in 2 Timothy 2:19b, ***"Let everyone who nameth the name of Christ depart from iniquity."***

The value and appreciation that you place on a name depend on the understanding that you have about that entity. So, what can we discover about the name of God from the scripture? Read along as we discover the greatness of his name.

The Power in His name.

"The name of the Lord is a strong tower, the righteous run into it and they are save" Proverbs 18:10.

"Wherefore God also hath highly exalted him, and given him a name which is above every name: That at the name of Jesus every knee should bow, of things in heaven, and things in earth, and things under the earth; And that every tongue should confess that Jesus Christ is Lord, to the glory of God the Father." Philippians 2:9-11

One of the attributes of God is the supreme power that his name holds. Thus, understanding the power in his name helps to define our relationship with him in the place of prayer. The recognition of that power also significantly contributes towards helping in building our confidence as we pray. The power in his name is not only recognized and revered by believers alone, even those belonging to the kingdom of darkness recognize the power and authority in his name. That is why the Lord encourages us to pray with his name.

"If ye shall ask any thing in my name, I will do it."
John   14:14

The authority that a powerful name commands can also be seen in the book of Nehemiah. Nehemiah was able to secure himself a safe passage from where he was living as a slave, to the land of his birth Jerusalem. This was because he carried a letter written by the authority of the name of the King. In addition, he also carried another letter by the King for others to provide him with the material that he needed to build.

"Moreover I said unto the king, if it please the king, let letters be given me to the governors beyond the river, that they may convey me over till I come into Judah; And a letter unto Asaph the keeper of the king's forest, that he may give me timber to make beams for the gates of the palace which appertained to the house, and for the wall of the city, and for the house that I shall enter into. And the king granted me, according to the good hand of my God upon me." Nehemiah   2:7-8 KJV

The power and authority which the name of the King bears was manifested in the seamless journey that Nehemiah made and neither did he face any shortage of wood to build. Do you realize that if Nehemiah had passed through territories sans the king's political influence, that letter would not have been acknowledged? So, if the name of an ordinary King commands so much power in his sphere of influence, what of the name of the King of kings. The one who rules over all the earth, whose kingdom knows no end? Remember, that is the name you are calling upon.

We also understand from the experience of the sons of Scevas that the kingdom of darkness also appreciates the power in the name of Jesus. That was why the evil spirit responded..... ***Jesus I know, and Paul I know, but who are ye? Acts 19:15***

You might wonder that these are all Biblical old stories. Does it have relevance in today's world? Oh yeah, these learning are very real and applicable even today. We can all appreciate the impact that our connection or relationship with those in authorities have on the opportunities that may come our way. The higher the name you are connected with, the bigger is the door of opportunities that opens for you. The good news is that the name of Jesus is higher than every other name, and thus with him your opportunities are unlimited.

"Wherefore God also hath highly exalted him, and given him a name which is above every name: That at the name of Jesus every knee should bow, of things in heaven, and things in earth, and things under the earth; And that every tongue should confess that Jesus Christ is Lord, to the glory of

God the Father,"
Philippians 2:9-11

Just like it is a privilege to know people in authority who can help you to move ahead in life. So it is with God. It is a privilege to be able to devoutly call on his name in prayers. That is why the songwriter wrote, *"what a privilege to carry, everything to God in prayer".*

As I conclude this section, I leave you with the word of the Lord in Mathew 28:18-20 that says.

"And Jesus came and spake unto them, saying, All power is given unto me in heaven and in earth. Go ye therefore, and teach all nations, baptizing them in the name of the Father, and of the Son, and of the Holy Ghost: Teaching them to observe all things whatsoever I have commanded you: and, lo, I am with you always, even unto the end of the world. Amen."

His Name is Holy

His holiness is one attribute of God that he wants to be guided jealously. He does not want to be associated with iniquity and indeed, he wants all who call upon his name appreciate the significance of his sanctity. That was why he said, **"be ye holy for I am holy."** This implies that for us to stand before him and call his name in prayers, with an expectation of results, we should honor Him in our daily living, by living a holy life.

I have found in my experience that the challenges faced by the majority in their prayer life today is not the ability to find time to pray, it is not the intensity of their prayers, it is not even the content of the prayers. The problem lies in the personality that is praying. Many of us fail to honor the name of God in our daily living and then blatantly come to the same God in prayers. That is why in the book of Isaiah 59, the Lord says.

"Behold, the Lord's hand is not shortened, that it cannot save; neither his ear heavy, that it cannot hear: But your iniquities have separated between you and your God, and your sins have hid his face from you, that he will not hear. For your hands are defiled with blood, and your fingers with iniquity; your lips have spoken lies, your tongue hath muttered perverseness. None calleth for justice, nor any pleadeth for truth: they trust in vanity, and

speak lies; they conceive mischief, and bring forth iniquity. They hatch cockatrice' eggs, and weave the spider's web: he that eateth of their eggs dieth, and that which is crushed breaketh out into a viper. Their webs shall not become garments, neither shall they cover themselves with their works: their works are works of iniquity, and the act of violence is in their hands. Their feet run to evil, and they make haste to shed innocent blood: their thoughts are thoughts of iniquity; wasting and destruction are in their paths. The way of peace they know not; and there is no judgment in their goings: they have made them crooked paths: whosoever goeth therein shall not know peace."
Isaiah 59:1-8 KJV

This scripture says it all. Iniquities limit the potentials in the place of prayer. From the thoughts in our hearts, the utterances from our mouth, our relationship with others, and the things that we do on a daily basis in our everyday lives; all these impact the effectiveness of our prayer life.

The Glory of His Name.

"Ascribe to the LORD the glory due his name; worship the LORD in the splendor of his holiness."
Psalm 29:2

Names do matter, and God's Name matters most of all. I still remember that when I had left my home for the first time to go to College, my parents called me and said, "Always remember your parents." It's a simple statement, but it carries so much weight and at that time it put so much responsibility on my young shoulders. For me, that statement meant, "It's not just about you, you represent a family, you are a bearer of a name that is held in honor. Go to College and defend that honor, defend your father's name. Do you know that if you don't honor your family name, you are invariably inviting dishonor to the name? What you do not value, even others will not appreciate."

Thus, while teaching us to pray, the Lord Jesus Christ wants us to understand that we are not only identifying with our Father in heaven, we have the huge responsibility to honor and bring honor to his name. I am sure you have been in situations when you may have heard others say, "Is he not a Christian? He should not have done that". In such instance, we have not brought honor to his name, to our Christian beliefs and our Christianity. Instead of lifting him up, we have brought disrepute to his name. But the scripture tells us that, if he is lifted up, he will draw all men to himself. And when he draws you to himself, you have access to all that he has in his bosom.

CHAPTER FIVE

THY KINGDOM COME

Thy Kingdom Come.... Get the priority right

"You ask and do not receive because you asked amiss"
James 4:3a.

To ask amiss means to ask wrongly or inappropriately. Even though the Lord has promised us that if we ask anything in his name, it shall be given unto us, this verse of the scripture goes a step further to emphasize the importance of asking for the right thing.

Can I ask you a question? As a child when you asked for something from your parents was it always given to you? If your parents were like mine, as indeed most parents, I guess the answer should be 'No'. They replied in negative not because they don't have the means, but because they either felt you don't need such a thing, or it is not yet the right time for you to have it. They understand and are aware that for then you need other important things and they will do everything within their means to provide it. It is bad parenting to acquiesce and give a child, everything he may desire even if it may destroy the child's life - all because you want to please the child. A child may argue that it is unfair to not receive what he wants, but at the same time, it is not fair for the parents to provide the child with something that is not good for the child's well-being. In other words, parents know best, and in the same vein, God, our heavenly father knows best for each of one of us.

Let me tell you this; God not only has the capacity to provide us with anything, but he also knows best what our needs are and fulfills them timely not before or after. If you ask of Him, in what is right, you will receive from him not anytime, but in his time, which is always the best and the right time.

One cannot attribute the failure to receive from God to not asking, but to not prioritizing our needs. Let me paint a scenario for you. Imagine a young farmer who is desirous of establishing his farming enterprise. He has identified and laid out all the basic requisites that he would need to be a successful farmer. He needs a farmland, farming tools and machinery, and seeds among others. Having ascertained all that is required, what do you think should be the first thing on his shopping list? My reasoning tells me that it should be the farmland. Do you agree with me? Imagine if the farmer would set out to look for the seeds first. I ask, where will the seeds be planted? What if he has the seeds and does not have the farmland to plant them after acquiring the seeds? The seed becomes useless. Apparently, he has not reflected properly on the proposition and has misrepresented his priorities on the list.

One of the fundamental teachings of the Lord's Prayer is to get our priorities right as we voice our request to the Lord. That is why the first request in the Lord's Prayer is "Let thy Kingdom come." That is priority number one and the most important prayer of all. In present times, the majority of Christians have misinterpreted this or not apprehended this and in doing so, have become limited in their prayer life. We are preoccupied and engrossed in asking Lord for the unimportant and inconsequential things while not contemplating enough on prioritizing our shopping list. The Lord further emphasized this as he engaged the Apostles.

"Therefore take no thought, saying, What shall we eat? or, What shall we drink? or, Wherewithal shall we be clothed? (For after all these things do the Gentiles seek:) for your heavenly Father knoweth that ye have need of all these things. But seek ye first the kingdom of God, and his righteousness; and all these things shall be added unto you."
Matthew   6:31-33

As simple as this prayer request seems on the surface, "Thy Kingdom Come," it is the most important request. It recognizes not only the personality of our God as a King over a kingdom, but it also demonstrates your understanding of your own personality as a Prince or Princess, as you are His son and this is vital for every believer.

If you are unaware of your position and rights, people will take advantage of you. And this is how the devil plays on our ignorance which can be exemplified from the beginning when he deceived Adam and Eve. You ask me how? Recall what he told Eve when he approached her in the Garden and encouraged her to eat of the fruit. "***And the serpent said unto the woman, Ye shall not surely die: For God doth know that in the day ye eat thereof, then your eyes shall be opened, and ye shall be as gods, knowing good and evil***". The devil wrongfully baited her as he said, "You shall be like Gods." Apparently, the idea of being like Gods sounded interesting to Eve, and she decided why not. But the truth is that when God made the man, he said: "Let us make man in our own image, after our own likeness". The truth is that she already was in His likeness and she was intending to be what she already was, but she never knew. She fell out with God, together with her husband because of lack of knowledge and clarity. No wonder the scripture says, "My people perish for lack of knowledge." The devil attempted the same method with the Lord Jesus Christ when he attempted to derail Jesus at the beginning of his Ministry. Let's recall that encounter for reference.

"Then was Jesus led up of the Spirit into the wilderness to be tempted of the devil. And when he

had fasted forty days and forty nights, he was afterward an hungred. And when the tempter came to him, he said, If thou be the Son of God, command that these stones be made bread. But he answered and said, It is written, Man shall not live by bread alone, but by every word that proceedeth out of the mouth of God. Then the devil taketh him up into the holy city, and setteth him on a pinnacle of the temple, And saith unto him, If thou be the Son of God, cast thyself down: for it is written, He shall give his angels charge concerning thee: and in their hands they shall bear thee up, lest at any time thou dash thy foot against a stone. [7] Jesus said unto him, It is written again, Thou shalt not tempt the Lord thy God. Again, the devil taketh him up into an exceeding high mountain, and sheweth him all the kingdoms of the world, and the glory of them;[9] And saith unto him, All these things will I give thee, if thou wilt fall down and worship me. [10] Then saith Jesus unto him, Get thee hence, Satan: for it is written, Thou shalt worship the Lord thy God, and him only shalt thou serve. [11] Then the devil leaveth him, and, behold, angels came and ministered unto him."

Look closely at what Satan said to Lord Jesus Christ in the first and the second tests, "If you are the son of God?" This question can be considered in two ways (1) You need to prove to me that you indeed are the son of God. (2) Do you have the power to make things happen? Jesus responded to basically tell him, "I know who I am, I have got nothing to prove to you about who I am, I know who I am and for that reason, I am not doing your bidding." Satan got the clear message and when he presented the third question to Jesus, he did not start with that question again. This is because he knew that Jesus Christ was not having an identity crisis. Thus, in his third attempt, all he told him was, "Surrender your Sonship, worship me, and I will give you the kingdom of the earth." Again, his response was, "You can't give me what belongs to me. The question is, do you know who you are?"

"But ye are a chosen generation, a royal priesthood, an holy nation, a peculiar people; that ye should show forth the praises of him who hath called you out of darkness into his marvelous light: Which in time past were not a people, but are now the people of God: which had not obtained mercy, but now have obtained mercy"

The devil continues in the business of performing this deceptive enterprise even today. Join me and say, ***May I not be a victim of his deception in Jesus name. Amen.***

Owing to our position in Christ, there are some things that we can access and we need not ask for them. This is because they have already been made available to you if indeed you are a child of the kingdom. But yet these things form the core of our prayer requests. That is why the scriptures say in Ecc 10:5-7.

"There is an evil I have seen under the sun, the sort of error that arises from a ruler: 6 Fools are put in many high positions, while the rich occupy the low ones. 7 I have seen slaves on horseback, while princes go on foot like slaves"

The importance of this prayer point can be better understood when we look at the life of the prodigal child as recorded in the scripture.

"And he said, A certain man had two sons: And the younger of them said to his father, Father, give me the portion of goods that falleth to me. And he divided unto them his living. And not many days after the younger son gathered all together, and took his journey into a far country, and there wasted his substance with riotous living. And when he had spent all, there arose a mighty famine in that land; and he began to be in want. And he went and joined himself to a citizen of that country; and he sent him into his fields to feed swine. And he would fain have filled his belly with the husks that the swine did eat: and no man gave unto him. And when he came to himself, he said, How many hired servants of my father's have bread enough and to spare, and I perish with hunger! I will arise and go to my father, and will say unto him, Father, I have sinned against heaven, and before thee, And am no

more worthy to be called thy son: make me as one of thy hired servants. And he arose, and came to his father. But when he was yet a great way off, his father saw him, and had compassion, and ran, and fell on his neck, and kissed him. And the son said unto him, Father, I have sinned against heaven, and in thy sight, and am no more worthy to be called thy son. But the father said to his servants, Bring forth the best robe, and put it on him; and put a ring on his hand, and shoes on his feet: And bring hither the fatted calf, and kill it; and let us eat, and be merry: For this my son was dead, and is alive again; he was lost, and is found. And they began to be merry."
Luke 15:11-24

Simply put, the request from the prodigal child is a prayer that says, "I reject the Kingdom of my father." This is in absolute and direct opposition of what the Lord's Prayer teaches us. What the prodigal child had failed to recognize was that he had access to a fortune because he was within his father's domain and under his watchful eyes. The moment he stepped out of that domain, the grace and the protection that he had been enjoying was withdrawn. This teaches us that whatever you are asking of the Lord, even if you receive it can only be sustained in his presence. Thus, it is critical that we desire to be in his kingdom at all time. Would you pray this prayer with me?

"Heavenly Father, let your eyes continually be upon me, let your grace not be withdrawn from my life. Let me continuously found joy in your Kingdom, in Jesus name." Amen.

With this understanding, let me ask, what have you petitioned for before God? Have you always been putting the cart before the horse? Do you have your priorities right in your prayer life? What quotient of your prayer is focused on the kingdom of God? To put yourself in the right perspective before God, you need to make the features of the God's Kingdom paramount in your life. And let me say this, God sees our heart. It is not about asking pretentiously for the Kingdom of God, but in reality indeed from the Kingdom we only desire things that can benefit us. This brings me to a key lesson that we can learn from the parable of the prodigal son.

The scriptures tell us that the prodigal son asked his Father, "Give me a portion that belongs to me." However, he never told the father that once he received it, he would be leaving his father. The request seemed as if he simply wanted to gain an understanding of his portion of the family fortune. This is exactly the challenge that the majority of Christians face today. We ask God for many things in prayers and the moment he answers us, we abandon him. Sometimes, we use it to even work against him. This happens when we literally forget about the Almighty God and start to worship what we have received by his grace. In the parable of the Prodigal Son, assuming the father had not given him his portion as requested, he may have thought his father to be wicked and assumed that the father does not like him. It is quite common to see a majority of Christians move away from God once they receive what they asked from him. Some people pray with all their heart and dedicate themselves to the service of God to relocate to another Country, State or City. To some others, it's a new job, a new car, marriage, and a child. In the process of praying for these things, they became a firebrand, calling heaven and earth down days and nights like in the days of Elijah. But the moment they get the desired answers, they become too sophisticated or busy to be a firebrand for Christ, and you know what the excuses are related to? They blame their laxity on what they have received from the Lord. Fellowship suddenly becomes a burden as it conflicts with their work schedules. The pressure of marital life suddenly becomes too much, making it acceptable to skip prayer meetings. The question is, should our relationship with God suffer because of what he has blessed us with?

Does these sounds familiar to you? Indeed, the Lord shared with us the parable of a prodigal son in the bible, but I can tell you that even today many such prodigal sons exist amongst us. And if I may ask, in the context of what you have read above, how do you consider yourself? Are you a prodigal child? Take a moment to reflect on that question. However, let me say this as I round up here; Kingdom living is our choice, the question is, are you ready for it?

Be Ready at All Times

Another key message that we may be able to grasp from praying for the 'Kingdom of God to come' is our desire to be ready for him, anytime he comes. Thus, by encouraging us to pray the Lord's Prayer, indirectly the Lord is asking us to pray about is being acceptable to him at all times. Considering that his coming according to the scripture is like a thief coming in the night, it means that there will be no prior notification of him coming at a particular time, it just requires that you are ready at all times. It is one thing for you to know about his coming, it is another for you to be fully prepared for his coming. That takes me to the parable of the ten virgins.

"Then shall the kingdom of heaven be likened unto ten virgins, which took their lamps, and went forth to meet the bridegroom. And five of them were wise, and five were foolish. They that were foolish took their lamps, and took no oil with them: But the wise took oil in their vessels with their lamps. While the bridegroom tarried, they all slumbered and slept. And at midnight there was a cry made, Behold, the bridegroom cometh; go ye out to meet him. Then all those virgins arose, and trimmed their lamps. And the foolish said unto the wise, Give us of your oil; for our lamps are gone out. But the wise answered, saying, Not so; lest there be not enough for us and you: but go ye rather to them

that sell, and buy for yourselves. And while they went to buy, the bridegroom came; and they that were ready went in with him to the marriage: and the door was shut. Afterward came also the other virgins, saying, Lord, Lord, open to us. But he answered and said, Verily I say unto you, I know you not. Watch therefore, for ye know neither the day nor the hour wherein the Son of man cometh."
Matthew   25:1-13

Inevitably, whenever I read this scripture, I start to meditate. It's a story of how a day that was meant for joy turned to sorrow and regret for some people. *I pray that your day of joy will not turn to a day of sorrow in Jesus name. Amen.* All the ten virgins achingly longed for this day to come and kept themselves pure to be qualified to receive the bridegroom. But yet, at the most crucial time, all those efforts became wasted.

Let us look at this scripture more closely. All the ten maidens had the basic qualification of virginity, which was an essential requirement to receive the bridegroom. To retain this quality, these ten bridegrooms would have faced a lot of challenges. They might have also sacrificed a lot of friendships and other opportunities, which they may have denied themselves to keep their purity intact. I could also imagine the pride of their parents on them being selected amongst all the maidens in the land.

The basic qualification here can be likened to receiving Christ as Lord and a personal savior and living a holy life. Will you also agree with me, that in the world today, this is not a popular position to be? Today in the commercially driven materialistic word there are variable kinds of pressure trying to get you out of the fold. In the process of starting on the right path, you may lose friends and indeed some opportunities that you would have loved to retain. But this is just the starting point, it does not mean you have reached your final destination. It may be relevant to your local Pastor that you are in the Church Directory as a regular and faithful member of your local congregation. Your name may be referenced very often as an example of a believer. But, does that mean that you are ready for his coming? Your name in the Church Directory does not guarantee you a place in the list in the Book of Life? God is not coming for those that are in the Church, he is coming for those that are not only in the Church, but are in Christ and are prepared for his coming.

I love the way the Message translation of the Bible put it in Mathew 7:21-23

"Knowing the correct password-saying 'Master, Master,' for instance-isn't going to get you anywhere with me. What is required is serious obedience-doing what my Father wills. I can see it now-at the Final Judgment thousands strutting up

to me and saying, 'Master, we preached the Message, we bashed the demons, our God-sponsored projects had everyone talking.' And do you know what I am going to say? 'You missed the boat. All you did was use me to make yourselves important. You don't impress me one bit. You're out of here."
Matthew 7:21-23

The five foolish virgins lost out not because they were evil, but because they were careless. Carelessness is the challenge of the majority of Christians today. If you are careless then you cannot blame anyone else if you are not ready when he comes. No wonder scriptures say we should work out our own salvation with fear and tremble. So, in that sense, you cannot blame the five wise virgins for refusing to give the foolish one's oil when they asked for it. I imagined that probably some of them would have been friends. They would have been chatting together while waiting for the arrival of the bridegroom. But when the bridegroom came, boundaries of the relationship were redefined. The denominational association to which you belong cannot guarantee you salvation, neither does your relationship with your Pastor.

"So then every one of us shall give account of himself to God."
Romans 14:12 KJV

It is important I also mention this as we look at the parable of the Ten Virgins. I want to believe that the five virgins that were ready would have loved to have their friends with them if possible. But, that could only have been possible if they had asked the right question at the right time. A simple question like, "Did you come along with extra oil," would have gotten a friend ready. Or could they have assumed that they should know? Yes, that could be it. That is the failure I have observed in Christian fellowship today. We all fall into the victim of this assumption that the other person knows what should be done. Even though we spend time with each other, but this time is mostly spent in discussing things irrelevant to the Kingdom of God. We need to be steadfast in encouraging one another. The real joy would be if we all make it to the end.

"But friends, you're not in the dark, so how could you be taken off guard by any of this? You're sons of Light, daughters of Day. We live under wide open skies and know where we stand. So let's not sleepwalk through life like those others. Let's keep our eyes open and be smart. People sleep at night and get drunk at night. But not us! Since we're creatures of Day, let's act like it. Walk out into the daylight sober, dressed up in faith, love, and the hope of salvation."

9-11 God didn't set us up for an angry rejection but for salvation by our Master, Jesus Christ. He died for us, a death that triggered life. Whether we're

awake with the living or asleep with the dead, we're alive with him! So speak encouraging words to one another. Build up hope so you'll all be together in this, no one left out, no one left behind. I know you're already doing this; just keep on doing it."
1 Thess. 5:4-11 (The Message)

He Will Not Impose Himself on You

"Behold, I stand at the door, and knock: if any man hear my voice, and open the door, I will come in to him, and will sup with him, and he with me."
Revelation 3:20 KJV

The request thy kingdom come also suggests that it is in our instance that he comes into our lives. The Lord would refrain from invading your space if you do not extend him an invitation. This is what he makes us understand in Revelations 3:20. You need to realize that when the prodigal child was to leave home, the father did not say, you cannot go, neither did he say, you have to leave behind everything I have given to you. The father allowed the prodigal son to go with everything. Now this is crucial. It was not the will of the father for the prodigal son to leave, but he allowed him to have his way. The fact that you received something that you requested in prayers does not necessarily mean that it is God's will for you to have it. The Prodigal Son received what he requested from his father, but that took him off course. That is why the next verse in the Lord's prayers says...Thy will be done on earth, as it is in heaven.

This brings me to the end of volume 1 of this book. In volume 2, we will be reviewing the rest of the Lord's Prayer, by asking the important question, **"How do I know His will?"**

God bless you.

ABOUT THE AUTHOR

Although born into an Islamic family, Toks converted to Christianity in 1995 and has been actively involved in the service of the Lord in different capacities since 1997. He pastored Parishes of RCCG in Nigeria before he relocated to Qatar in 2006 on a secular appointment. His passion for souls and impactful service to the community came alive again while in Qatar and with the help of God, he pioneered the establishment of the first Parish of RCCG in Qatar in 2007. While in Qatar, he also facilitated the planting of RCCG Parishes in Pittsburgh USA and Lusaka Zambia. Toks relocated to Canada in 2013 on another secular assignment and true to his nature and passion for Church planting, he led the team to start RCCG Rehoboth Assembly in Calgary in December 2013

A prolific writer and teacher of the word, his writings have been a source of inspiration and blessing to many over the years. His blog site (@Pastor Toks) also provides another platform for reaching out to soul across all borders.

Married to his best friend and Prayer Partner, Adewumi, they are blessed with four lovely girls, Ike, Eni, Ife and Ewa.

Made in the USA
Charleston, SC
03 January 2017